LINDA CONNOR
SPIRAL JOURNEY

Photographs 1967-1990

For Dana
I hope we will see
each other again in San Francisco.
All the best, Linda Connor

Preface By

Denise Miller-Clark

Introduction By

Rebecca Solnit

The Museum Of Contemporary Photography

Columbia College Chicago

Front cover: *Lotus, Kashmir, India, 1985*

ISBN 0-932026-21-4
Library of Congress Catalogue Card
Number 90-60331

Designed by Mary Johnson.
Phototypeset in Bembo and Bembo Italic.
Printed on Lustro Dull Enamel by Rohner
Printing Company in Chicago, Illinois.

The Museum Of Contemporary
Photography was founded in 1984 by
Columbia College Chicago as a natural
outgrowth of the Chicago Center for
Contemporary Photography, established
in 1976, to exhibit, collect and promote
contemporary photography. The
Museum is unique in the Midwest for its
exclusive commitment to the medium
and is the product of the long-held
reputation that Columbia College
Chicago enjoys as an institution which
provides the public with superior
programs in the teaching and exhibiting
of photography. Programs of the
Museum include a Permanent Collection
and Print Study Room, a series of lectures
and panel discussions, membership
benefits, a Museum Studies Program,
sponsored by the Columbia College
Chicago Department of Photography,
publications, and traveling exhibitions
originated by the Museum.

The Museum Of Contemporary
Photography is accredited by the
American Association of Museums.

This publication accompanies a traveling
exhibition of the work of Linda Connor
prepared by The Museum Of
Contemporary Photography. For
information, contact Denise Miller-
Clark, Director, The Museum Of
Contemporary Photography, Columbia
College Chicago, 600 South Michigan
Avenue, Chicago, Illinois 60605-1996.

Linda Connor: Spiral Journey
The Museum Of
Contemporary Photography
13 April through 30 May 1990

I first came to know the breadth of Linda Connor's work through a slide presentation. As I listened to the tantric choir of the Gyoto monks, I watched the images dissolve, echo and resonate: megalithic dolmens into volcanic terrain, Inca ruins, ancient ceremonial caves, mountain vistas, carved and inscribed rocks (petroglyphs), winding rivers, canyons and waterfalls, antlers and twisted branches, prayer flags, monks, veiled women and musicians, carved head and footprints of the Buddha. Each new image retained a remembrance of the previous one, added meaning and suggested interconnectedness. T.S. Eliot perhaps first observed that every major work of art forces upon us a reassessment of all previous works.

Preface

A THOUSAND EFFECTS

Although in essence it is single,
it hath a thousand effects: innumerable
names befit that one thing.

Rūmī, Mathnawī

It was after the slide presentation that I realized Linda Connor is not simply a landscape photographer. She is a photographer of the land and its people, nature and culture. Since 1967 she has traveled to distant and familiar places on six continents and a few islands. While no complete written journal may illuminate for us her experiences—for though Connor admires journal-keeping but writes "Most evenings, rather than recounting the day's adventures, I am ensconced in the towel-draped closet of my room, reloading film holders"—Rebecca Solnit's introduction to this book provides insight into the photographer and the qualities of her photographs, her influences and the ideas that shape her work—a spiral journey.

In a previous article on the artist, Rebecca Solnit observed, "Seen as a whole…her work reveals a pilgrimage toward a kind of spiritual home, a place of bare earth, religious architecture, cultures stretching back in time, of myths and sacred presences." Connor's images possess an animated force beyond that which is photographed. Her work is not only about temporal situations; the images honor the subjects with uncritical attention, but they are most often timeless, symbolic, iconographic. Connor writes, "I have always gravitated toward images that reveal the 'essence' of something, the apparition of a form or idea, rather than a particular fact." Her subjects take on a strong, vivid presence—as a critic recently put it, a "delicate terror." For although the images are clear and not manipulated, they reach for a significance that goes beyond a photographic document. Hence, there is no concrete singular meaning that the viewer must "get" upon viewing her photographs. In fact as her work matures, the photographer finds new meanings for her photographs, new understandings of them. The new ones do not cancel any other readings of these works; the meanings are merely compounded.

Over the years, Linda Connor's work has evolved into an investigation of the visual forms of the sacred. To that end, she simply followed her intuitions. She says, "I am curious about the way a stone can be transformed by marks or by placement to then function as a sacred object." Of ancient rock art, she concludes, "I've come to believe that often the drawings were done to channel and mitigate the awe one feels in response to the powers of the surrounding universe." The photographer is challenged by how she can use a machine to describe the indescribable by use of composition and symmetry, by altering the spacial representations of things, by using extreme clarity, the grace of light, and attention that honors the things photographed.

Linda Connor's single images have a quiet potency. This potency is amplified when they are put into sequence. "By definition," writes Kubler in *The Shape of Time,* "a formal sequence exceeds the capacity of any individual to exhaust its possibilities in one lifetime. [She] can nevertheless imagine more than [s]he can execute." The sequencing of Connor's

FIGURE 1

*Hennaed Hand
Nepal, 1980*

and viewers' continued approaches with "Although in essence it is single, it hath befit that one thing."

Linda Connor have made an impact on Born in New York in 1944, she began Callahan at the Rhode Island School of and Arthur Siegal at the Institute of where she received her Master of Science photography primarily at the San workshop and lecture centers throughout

work may be reformulated by the artist's different but equally meaningful results. a thousand effects: innumerable names

The photographs and ideas of contemporary American photography. her photographic education under Harry Design, and later under Aaron Siskind Design at Illinois Institute of Technology degree in 1969. Since then she has taught Francisco Art Institute and at many the United States.

Linda Connor has been the recipient of National Endowment for the Arts Individual Artist Grants in 1976 and 1988, the John Simon Guggenheim Memorial Foundation Fellowship in 1979, the Friends of Photography Photographer of the Year Award in 1986 and the Charles Pratt Memorial Foundation Award in 1988. She has been involved in numerous group exhibitions and has had many one-woman shows. This publication documents a mid-career retrospective of photographs made between the years 1967 and 1990, the only representation of the photographer's work as a whole, and the first major book since her 1979 monograph *Solos*.

This book would have been impossible to produce without the kind assistance of many individuals and the cooperation of many institutions. Most importantly, I would like to thank Linda Connor for her photographs and her vision, for her physical energy, durable health and powers of concentration, for the enthusiasm and dedication with which she has participated in all aspects of this project. I would also like to thank Rebecca Solnit for her insightful text from which the title for the book and exhibition is derived.

Linda Connor would like to thank the following for their generous support of her work over the years: the John Simon Guggenheim Memorial Foundation, the National Endowment for the Arts and the Charles Pratt Memorial Foundation. In particular, she wishes to thank Harry Callahan and Aaron Siskind for their teachings, encouragement and inspiration that their lives as working artists provided. A special thanks is extended to Aaron for generously providing the funds for a companion to accompany her on her 1988 trip to Asia. Jean McMann on that venture and Andrew Roth on the 1989 journey to Egypt and Israel are commended for their patience and humor in the smooth and rough times working in a third world environment. Jack Deardorff is offered a long overdue thank you for his kindness in arranging for an 8x10 from his workshop to be sent to her when her Deardorff was stolen in Thailand in 1979 on her first extended trip to Asia; he really saved that trip and a number of the images in this book would not have been made without that replacement camera. Most importantly, Linda thanks her family and friends whose love and encouragement is immeasurable.

At The Museum Of Contemporary Photography, assistant director Ellen Ushioka, curatorial assistant and preparator Martha Alexander-Grohmann, and all museum interns were instrumental in preparing the exhibition for its presentation in Chicago and its subsequent tour, and the documentation and cataloguing of photographs for this book. I am grateful for their tireless devotion to standards of excellence. And toward that same realm, I am appreciative of the skillful talents of graphic designer Mary Johnson who organized the material into its elegant form. Thanks must also go to Rudy Rohner and the staff of Rohner Printing in Chicago for their commitment to reproducing Linda Connor's photographs with such great fidelity.

The exhibition and publication programs of The Museum Of Contemporary Photography have been enthusiastically supported by John Mulvany, Chairman of the Museum Governing Board, President Mike Alexandroff and Executive Vice President Bert Gall of Columbia College Chicago, and the College's Board of Trustees.

The publication of this book and the preparation of the exhibition for its national tour were aided by grants to The Museum Of Contemporary Photography from the National Endowment for the Arts, a federal agency, the Illinois Arts Council, a state agency, and the Institute of Museum Services, a federal agency that offers general operating support to the nation's museums.

Denise Miller-Clark, *Director*
The Museum Of Contemporary Photography

Accredited by the American Association of Museums

Long before the trees grew up, the stone head must have been part of a statue, the statue must have been tended and worshipped, the worshippers must have been part of a culture that abandoned it so long ago that the roots had time to grow up around this relic, to embrace it indifferently as prelude to engulfing it. After the tree and the head grew together, the lichen came and treated them as though they were the same, and if the tree is indifferent to the sacredness of the statue, the statue seems equally unconcerned about its fate. The serene smile of the head remains, and its compelling presence as a sacred object hasn't worn away as the details and the smoothness of its features have. The tree's base and the statue's head fill the photograph so that nothing can be seen beyond; the wholly sacred and the wholly natural are all that is visible [Figure 2 and Plate 33].

Spiral Journey

THE SEVENTH

DIRECTION

"The six directions can meet only in lived time, in the place people call home, the seventh direction, the center."

Ursula K. LeGuin

needs no critical explanation, an image setting that might attract the camera of a straightforward image, a gift to us of saw, and at first only the limpid clarity mysterious darknesses, set it apart as than any other denomination of travel Linda Connor, one of hundreds of 8x10 dozen years, and seen as part of this

In some ways this is a photograph that of a curious conjunction in an exotic any traveler who happened upon it. It is a marvelous sight the photographer and deep shadows, the evocation of the work of an artist, as art rather photography. But the photograph is by contact prints she has made in the last larger body of work, it becomes

epigrammic, a summary of some of the qualities and ideas that shape her work.

Connor has often been called a landscape photographer, and though a profound connection to the natural world is manifested in her work, the term falls short in describing it. There are images that are landscapes by any standard, but there are also images of temples, of the interiors of caves, of standing stones, veiled women, petroglyphs, animals, musicians. To be a landscape photographer has a prerequisite: to define the landscape as a distinct and separate subject. Connor has photographed the land as part of the continuum of being, and her work is centered upon the territory in which the human and the natural connect and where cultures have connected with the sacred. The sacred, the natural: time is the third distinct theme of her works, and the image described above is a touchstone, a point of entry for understanding all three.

American photography established landscape as a certain kind of ideal, a zone whose virginity implied its ripeness for conquest, untouched land waiting for its explorers and explored visually by the photographer, proxy for the viewer and for the burgeoning culture. More recently, photographers began documenting the incursions of Americans into the landscape, showing buildings so ugly, sensibilities so blunted that, by implication, untouchedness was the only viable state for landscape. Connor approaches from a vastly different point of view, and her photographs don't adhere to the American sense of mankind as a recent trespasser in the natural world. Her images aren't waiting for explorers; the space may be full or impenetrable or already long inhabited. The stone head in the photograph is older than the trees, and the culture that made it seems to have abandoned it and vanished: this is a picture of a place where culture is ancient and the natural world is powerful, powerful enough to overwhelm the artifacts of human activity.

Several kinds of time are interlaced here: the sacred timelessness of the gods, of which the smile is a reminder, the long-ago linear time of ancient history, the cyclical, regenerative time of nature, and the daily cycle of changing light so crucial to the making of photographs. In this scheme of time, the identifying materials of the present are more often than not merely distraction, like static on the radio, like gnats, something to be banished for the sake of clarity. A similar sense of layered times, sacred presences and natural life is present in many other images: of petroglyphs incised into the flat rock foreground of a Hawaiian landscape tufted with dry grass [Plate 26]; or a stone basin in India whose carved footprints of the Buddha are filled with water in which blossoms float [Figure 3]; or of a pile of horns in the foreground of a crumbling temple in the Himalayas [Plate 38].

FIGURE 2

Entwined Buddha
Ayuthaya, Thailand, 1988

These three themes—nature, time, the sacred—emerge clearly only in the most recent body of work, the vast ongoing series of 8x10 contact prints, but this oeuvre extends a more basic subject that could be considered the crux of all her work since her undergraduate days in Rhode Island. It could be called centers, nexuses, focal points, the places—on whatever scale—where things have been brought together to evoke or celebrate the power and meaning of life, where experience intensifies. Educated in the Bauhaus tradition and influenced by the documentary photography of the FSA, Connor initially strove to portray the social conditions that had been the FSA's concern. Within the boundaries of that tradition, she began to move toward a more personal, subjective response to the visual world around her. Her own concerns are clear in one of the earliest works in the exhibition, the scene of a bureau top piled with belongings [Plate 1]. The mirror, which might tell us who the author of this composition is or where we are—the documentary facts—reflects only the pale expanse of wall and ceiling. The truth conveyed is wholly the creation of the unseen subject: the identity defined by a funeral parlor calendar with its image of Jesus, a collection of family photographs from various times and a cluster of medicine jars. This is where the room's inhabitant has concentrated the objects that give her life meaning; it is a secular shrine as well as an oblique portrait.

Connor cites Walker Evans as an important early influence, and she clearly learned more than a certain kind of documentary subject matter from his work—or was attracted to him for the aspects of his sensibility that transcend the documentary. Like Connor, Evans had a talent for recognizing how others endow their worlds with meaning and how the arrangements of inanimate objects around them may speak more eloquently of their lives than even their faces. His photographs are saturated with a kind of monumental stillness, an almost nineteenth-century sense of the pose, of letting the subject present itself with all its dignity, rather than, as photographic terminology has it, "be captured" in a spontaneous moment. This static quality, the fruit of an unhurried, respectful encounter between artist and subject, is central to Connor's work, as is the kind of vernacular iconization which Evans—and for that matter, Atget—give their subjects. The latter perhaps results from a compositional strategy that centers the subject as though to enshrine it, but does so without the rigidity, the perfect symmetry and flattening frontality of the wholly formal. The subject is given something of the icon's concentrated power without being severed from its surroundings.

Connor moved from Rhode Island to Chicago to attend graduate school there, and she found her documentary work difficult to continue in the strife-torn vastness of Chicago at the end of the sixties. Her subject shifted from photographs arranged in others' homes to her own arrangements of photographs, from documentary to an almost surrealist kind of invention—though the gap between the bureau-portrait and the collaged photographs isn't as vast as the categories suggest. Connor had been photographing photographs as a way of examining not facts but the construction of meaning. She had also been accumulating a large number of old photographs of strangers that, with her own family portraits, became the source material for the new work. In one image [Plate 2], a triple portrait rests on a rumpled bed, telescoping times and degrees of reality as would such later portraits as the stone head in the tree roots. (It isn't necessary to know that the bed is in Connor's grandmother's house or that the triptych is of her parents and herself, but the knowledge clarifies the sense of layered times and ties.)

The making of set-ups progressed, and she began creating compositions entirely out of existing two-dimensional images. The results are magical and confusing, playing with the photograph's tendency to eradicate distinctions between the real and the represented. A duo marches toward us, their heads obscured by photographs, their bodies adorned with foliage and their burden transformed into another photograph, this one of a beaming couple—her parents—from another era than their bearers [Plate 5]. A pair of uniformed men and a girl in a white first-communion dress stand like billboards in a landscape that is, we later realize, only a picture the portraits lie upon [Plate 7]. The talismanic power of photography was the implicit subject of these images, the dawning recognition of a power encapsulated in the later work. The experiments grow: a real chambered nautilus lies next to a book plate of Weston's nautilus photograph; St. Veronica's miraculous veil is overlaid with leaves; a print of Boticelli's Birth of Venus is enhanced— or defaced—by the addition of real shells whose scale and dimensionality undermine the coherent reality of the painting as a window into another world [Plate 9]. The objects placed on these prints and photographs celebrate and pay homage to them, as offerings do, at the same time that they debunk the illusion that they are anything more than flat objects. In this respect they foreshadow the more recent photographs, which return to a more documentary approach and continue the investigation of the sacred. In neither the early nor the late work is belief a precondition for reverence.

Similarly, the anonymity of the people in the found photographs was not a barrier to her involvement with them; their mystery reflected Connor's own mystery as an adopted child whose biological parents remained unknown until many years later. "Once it was made conscious, the power went out of it," she says of her realization that the portrait-collages constituted an exploration of her own veiled past and lost biological family. In the contemporary work made in traditional cultures and sacred sites around the world, a similar situation prevails: Connor's sense of connection to these places does not undo her identity as an outsider, and so no one place holds her but many lure

her. It is as though she recognizes the bonds of membership. The soft- 1979 book *Solos* was a venture outside and belonging, into a realm of powerful connection underlaid the with her Great Aunt Ethelyn's pictorialist era. A gift to Connor Ethelyn's camera became a gift of the world, of a purely photographic by the peculiarities of the lense.

FIGURE 3

Buddha's Footprints
India, 1979

a poetic affinity that transcends focus work that culminated in the these issues of information pure presence. In another way, a photographs—they were all taken specially made portrait lense from the from her aunt and uncle, Aunt this soft, luminous way of seeing vision, a way of seeing made possible

Ethelyn's portrait lense imbued objects with a presence Connor before and since has tried to locate in the things themselves. The more recent photographs testify to an ongoing quest for the places and things that manifest sacred power—though the recognition that the sacred constitutes a central theme came to her long after it was established in the images. The quest for meaning, belonging present in all the work focuses and deepens as the pursuit of the sacred. For the believer, a sacred site is the center of the world, the end of the journey; for Connor, each site is a center, and the journey has pauses but no end (and it should be remembered that her role as an outsider is not only cultural or the position of an adoptee, but the place of artists in any culture). She has taken her view camera to Ireland, France, Hawaii, Peru, the American southwest, Nepal, India, Egypt, Thailand, to the scattered places where the past still has a powerful presence and the land a kind of stark majesty, to a thousand centers. For the modern traveler a journey is about going away, an escape; the scope and persistence of Connor's travels suggest the pilgrim's sense of direction is more apt, the journey as return, as circular (or spiraling) rather than linear. In fact the circular and the linear become a crucial dialectic in her work: the circle of cyclical natural and ceremonial time versus the line of historical progress, the circle which makes the journey outward culminate in arrival at the starting point, the circle of containment, of centering, for the center is her enduring subject.

Connor said in 1988, "From the Paleolithic to the present, evidence exists of elegant and intelligent attempts to link human experience to the rhythms and forces of the universe. Now, facing a future whose very existence is in question, it becomes crucial to challenge the myopia of linear progress because of its failure to perceive the infinite round of being." Her work always has a quality of *homing in,* of arriving at a place that becomes home in some sense, fulfillment ("to an ultimate objective," says the dictionary, "to a successful or rewarding end"). Mircea Eliade, in his speculations on sacred space, writes that the sacred breaks up the homogeneity of the world, giving it definition and meaning, at the same time that the sacred reveals a reality opposed to the unreality of its surroundings. The sacred, in his view, gives those who recognize it identity, belonging, a point of reference, "an absolute fixed point, a center."

THE LAND
HERSELF

The idea of journey as return can be linked to that of the female earth. In *Nature and Madness,* Paul Shepard writes, "Sigmund Freud believed, for example, that the psychical foundation of all travel was the first separation and the various other departures from one's mother, including the final journey into death. Journeying is therefore an activity related to a larger feminine realm, so that it is not surprising that Freud himself was ambivalent about it. Of the landscape he said, 'All of these dark woods, narrow defiles, high grounds and deep penetrations are unconscious sexual imagery, and we are exploring a woman's body.'" Connor points out that mythological journeys are largely masculine, that women are archetypically more often concerned with familiar ground than terra incognita, and her own journeys are an expansion of that involvement with home, for something other than the Other of travel.

Sacred places become landmarks, a means of giving definition to the terrain, a spiritual geography. Connor has approached the issue of meaning in landscape from another perspective, which is equally important to understanding her work: feminism and identity rooted in gender. As she herself put it at a 1982 conference: "Concerning the myth of our relationship to land in Western culture, we can—despite its complexities—put it briefly: Man feels estranged from nature and his environment. The Fall, the expulsion from Eden. This estranged nature was associated with woman (also seen as "other") and her generative ability. Nature was seen as a female alien force, attracting and terrifying to men. They are forever trying to conquer and control it [or, she adds now, be seduced by it] rather than see themselves as part of it. Terms like virgin territory, Mother Nature, Mother Earth all speak clearly of this association. The relationship of women to the land is basically different. It is internalized and incorporated into the individual life—the challenge aspect is not a driving force. Women define territory and protect it by their presence and their experience; absent is the need to explore, transcend, and possess....Women have territory also. It's strongly felt and expressed. We are nature, so why venture very far? The territory of women tends to be the place we occupy, rather than the search for new places and spaces."

Connor has described women's landscape imagery as often being intimate in scale, domestic in geography: close-ups, scenes of gardens and locations close to home, places given meaning by experience. Traditional landscape art, first as painting, then as photography, has persistent characteristics that seem tied to masculine experience. From its emergence as a separate genre in the seventeenth century, landscape painting was often a vehicle for nationalism, a celebration of ownership or a report on explorations of exotic terrain. The fulfillment of these agendas often takes the form of the prospect (a term which means both an extensive view and financial expectations), of landscape as property. The far-reaching vantage point serves a sense of objectivity, of command over an expanse. When photographic technology made landscape photography possible in the second half of the last century, painting dictated many of its formal aspects, and its functions further determined its form. The prospect gave way to the survey, the

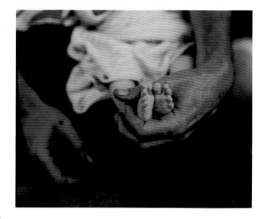

FIGURE 4

Baby Feet
1978

investigation of unfamiliar lands as settlement. Connor's idea of space becomes a means of reassessing the composition, in which natural frame an open space that is an a void waiting to be entered. This a staple of conventional landscape foregrounds of images from the Gossage, Richard Misrach and many a counterpoint, a depiction of and unyielding landscape. Connor interlaced branches, thickets, close-

a prelude to their development and as masculine, place as feminine here usual renaissance-perspective objects—rocks, mountains, trees— invitation to the explorer/viewer, spaciousness has remained photography. (The clotted seventies by Lee Friedlander, John more photographers are forbidden zones, of impenetrable has made her share of images of up ground and cliff faces, and her

open landscapes contain paths, roads, ruins—signs that the landscape is already full of eventfulness, not waiting for it.)

Spaciousness might be one of the gauges for distinguishing landscape from still life; in traditional work we can usually tell one from the other, in Connor's work the distinctions blur. Perhaps it's that place is somewhere between space and the still-life subject; neither a void nor an object, it is extensive, but possessed of an identity. Landscape began in Western art as the stage set for human dramas, and the perspectives in which it was depicted emphasized this quality, even after the actors disappeared (in the seemingly uninhabited American landscape, the scene is at the beginning of the play, the actors with their ploughs and guns are in the wings). To make the stage so fully the subject eliminates the possibility of other dramas, makes the landscape its own drama, a substance rather than a surface. And when the emphasis shifts from surface to substance, meaning becomes something inherent in the subject rather than an effect of composition. Frederick Sommer clarified the space-place distinction when he photographed the Arizona desert as a perspectiveless tapestry, a thing to be contemplated rather than a space to be entered. This is the land not on our terms but on its, and it is emphatically a portrait of land, not of the traversible space above it. In the seventies, as Connor was beginning her 8x10 series, the photographs of the earth from outer space had a tremendous impact. For the first time the planet was seen as an island of life, a closed system, an entity. This view terminated the boundless newness crucial to the century of American landscape that had come before. Connor's own break with renaissance perspective has less to do with Sommer's investigation of philosophical and formal issues than with the apprehension of sacred time through sacred land. Flattened landscapes, she says, squeeze out linear progress.

Connor has made an enormous variety of landscapes, from classic grassland vistas to tightly framed scenes of fresh lava flows. One unusual quality that emerges from the viewing of a quantity of her works is her sensuous appreciation of the earth as an entity itself. She very often photographs in places where the land is bare of grass and the other coverings that soften and disguise it, in deserts and arid lands, in the heights of mountains, at volcanos, on the edges or into the faces of cliffs, the mouths and interiors of caves. Like Sommer's landmark photographs, these images often depict a horizonless, perspectiveless landscape that entirely fills the picture plane. The surfaces visible in these images imply the vast geology beyond them, as a close-up of a bit of human anatomy might imply the whole body, and the intricate textures of cliff face or water-carved stone slope recall microphotographic images of living tissue. One appeal of these arid lands is the sense of vast, slow time that they convey, another is their function as parts of a whole that is the earth itself. Scenes of forests and grassy meadows convey a biological reality, a seasonally changing ecosystem of relatively brief lifespans; scenes of rock and soil speak of geological time, of years in the millions and billions, of the lifespan of the planet.

Often the photograph Connor makes is clearly a detail of a larger whole: stones from a vast wall, a carved stone inside a tomb, a swath of lava. Many of the images also suggest the earth as a vast body, as the ancient matriarch of early religion; these are the images of caves, rifts, fissures, valleys and other enclosed, intimate spaces and openings. In one potent image, light gleams on water that ripples around an islet of dark rocks in midstream, and dark rocks fill the rest of the image. This is an apprehension of the maternal earth in the purely natural. In another image, the lava that long ages ago ran hot had cooled and hardened in a cave to form a vast labial shape; here the Hawaiians had once worshipped Pele, the goddess of the volcano, before the location was forgotten, and so a cultural interpretation overlays the natural [Plate 36]. (It is, incidentally, one of many images that have stories about their making. In finding her subject matter, Connor has taken on some of the roles of an ethnologist or anthropologist; many of her sites are found through locals' word-of-mouth or have stories about them that she collects. In some ways the art constitutes only one facet of an ongoing involvement with these places and cultures. Connor often collects ritual objects and artworks made by the local peoples and lives in an environment that is itself residue or evidence of her travels. She reads extensively about the mythologies and other cultural creations of the communities she works in—and although it is not necessary to be able to identify, for example, the various deities in the petroglyphs to look at her photographs of them, it does put the work in a slightly different light to know that she can.)

Her reverence for the earth, like that of many contemporary feminists and ecologists, has affinities to the earth-worship of earlier cultures, and the ties between respect for the earth and earth-based matriarchal cultures discussed by Lucy Lippard, Merlin Stone and many others have contributed to her understanding of the issues. Both the identity of the sacred and the role of women are fundamentally different in cultures where the earth is sacred, where sanctity is liable to be here rather than beyond, where the spiritual and the material are less a duality, where the generative processes are held in awe and the natural cycle of growth and decay isn't seen as a falling off from former perfection. Most of her landscapes contain signs of such earlier cultures, from the art of petroglyphs in the southwest to the ruins of Macchu Picchu in Peru or the standing stones of Brittany. In these images the subject is as much the response of an earlier people to a place as the place itself (it could be considered art about art in an unorthodox way). These touched landscapes layer meanings and realities, somewhat like the early experimental work of images within images did: the interwoven with the geological and cyclical times of a place, a past in which someone responded to the site as special, perhaps sacred. Connor's interpretation, her choice and framing, becomes the last and most recent round in a long cycle of events.

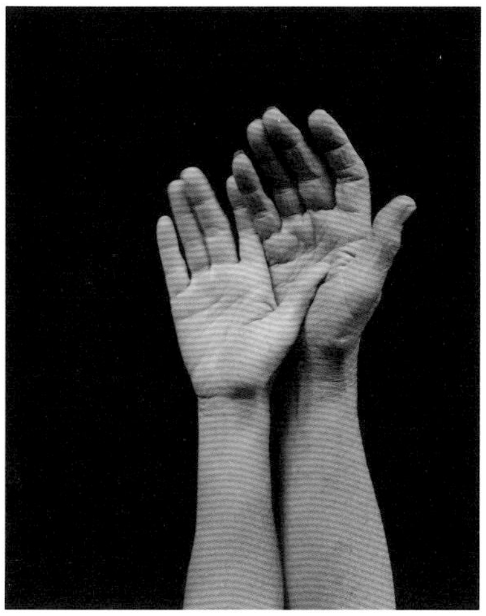

FIGURE 5

My Hand With My Mother's
1987

Too, the petroglyphs and stones and temples are about a presentation of information, so Connor becomes a participant in the act of making visible by photographically extending that visibility. Much photography has sought out that which is oblivious to its potential as an image, to its appearance and its meaning—"pure" nature, people unaware of the camera, spontaneous occurrences and chance encounters. Connor's human subjects are always invited participants in the act of making their portrait, they pose and look at the photographer. Altars are also about presentation. And on a more intimate scale, Connor has used hands to make presentations, and the hand is a recurrent motif in her work. In an early image, a hand wears a pearly shell on one finger. In *Solos*, a hand caresses a foot [Plate 15], and in a more recent piece, a weatherbeaten hand nestles the tiny feet of a newborn baby [Figure 4]. A woman's hand painted with henna patterns is extended toward a pair of statues [Figure 1]. And when Connor found her biological family a few years ago, she made a portrait of her hand and her mother's hand reaching in the same direction [Figure 5], and another one of her three half-siblings' hands and her hand together, a knot of kinship [Figure 6].

Connor likes patterns, from the patterns of stacked bones in the catacombs in Paris to the formal-garden patterns of Persian carpets to the interlocking spirals incised on megalithic stones in Ireland. Patterns suggest a complex order, a whole that unites the parts. Rather than repeat the pattern by documenting their totality, however, she often homes in on a detail, a corner or microcosm that implies the whole. Her images suggest fragments gathered from a scattering of times and places. In groups the work manifests its own patterns—the fragments are pieced together as part of Connor's larger pattern. In a recent small group of images the artist chose for an exhibition, the echos and refrains were startlingly rich. A Paleolithic cave and a subterranean-looking shrine to the Madonna; the elongated lines of the robes of the jamb figures on Chartres Cathedral's west facade and the curving lines of an ancient land-maze in California; this fragment of Native American maze and a detail of the maze inlaid into the nave floor at Chartres; these mazes and the delicate lines of the death figures drawn on a temple wall in Nepal; all the shadowy interiors and the cave of Pele; Pele and the Madonna; a series of small handprint outlines on a cliff face in Utah, looking frail and imploring. Together these images begin to suggest the immense tapestry of human birth and death, of the wombs and tombs that precede and follow upon life, of the recurrent patterns of an immense journey made up of journeys, a picture put together by Connor's own picturemaking journeys.

The discovery of vast patterns in the natural world has been one of the most significant advances in the natural sciences in recent times. Western thinking from the scientific revolution onward tended to regard the earth as a chaos of disconnected bits, and this sense of meaninglessness licensed much of the tampering and conquering of nature by scientists, governments and individuals. Some of the patterns were there to see for those who looked carefully, for mystics, traditional and rural peoples, for Thoreau, for John Muir (who said, "Whenever we try to pick out anything by itself we find it hitched to everything else in the universe."). Larger patterns became perceptible with the development of attitudes and equipment that could encompass vast times and places: the Gaia hypothesis, in which the earth can be understood as a self-regulating entity is one, the revelations of chaos theory about weather patterns and biological cycles are among the others. The emerging ideas of scientists and ecologists about an inherent interconnected order are part of a larger transformation of understanding in which artists have participated. Landscape photography particularly has had a tremendous resurgence in the past fifteen years, and in its emphasis on the politics and spirituality of landscape, it differs from most modernist landscape. The land no longer serves as a conceptual vacation from human issues, but as the crux of them; nature and culture are profoundly interdependent. Connor's work was eloquently describing this sense of pattern and connection as the newfound awareness was emerging, and her photographs are one of the strongest and most extensive essays on it.

A Handful
Of Dust

A photograph is a tacit contract between eternity and a moment, an enduring image of a brief conjunction of objects, an event, a condition of light that perhaps lasted only so long as the shutter was open. The camera is not a stand-in for the eye, but another way of seeing, and Connor's images remind us that this is so.

H ers is an intuitive approach to making photographs, based more on response than imposition. It could be said that she is more interested in Pele's cave than in Plato's cave, in the immediacy of the sacred rather than the analyses of philosophy. Running through all the work is a quality of openmindedness, of seeing each thing anew rather than conceptualizing it as still life, portrait or landscape. Because of dyslexia, the artist learned to read unusually late by the standards of the culture, and it could be postulated that the abstracting, distancing and generalizing effects of written language have been less a part of her perception than most of ours. A Fluxus artist once remarked that some distinctions are very important to make and others are very important not to make. In Connor's work, the differences between the neolithic and the gothic, between Nepal and Arizona, between nature and culture are deemphasized, and the affinities, the enduring, encompassing sensibility is investigated. The multiplicity of experience is in balance with the unity of its essence. Hindu myths come to mind, or of Krishna's thousands of gopis: the idea of the

FIGURE 6

Family
1988

Brahma's ten thousand incarnations simultaneous dalliance with myriad forms of the one.

T he sense of interconnectedness the mythic realm, in which gods take spirits, humans are turned into stones walk about, in which all distinctions in Nepal: "On market days the around the larger temples and forming one more frieze of life to the temple. I imagined with

of nature and culture calls to mind the form of animals, places have or trees, animals speak wisely, trees are permeable. She writes of her time women and children would gather monuments to set out their produce, add to the round of beings encircling amusement a frustrated Jesus attempting to dislodge the woman with her apricots and onions from the temple stairs." Although Connor has made no image of this scene, it suggests one of her 8x10 contact prints: the business of survival and the celebration of the sacred going on together in a culture more geared towards continuums than compartments, that likewise doesn't make rigid distinctions.

T he camera makes its own distinctions, however. A stream flows straight at us in a stony landscape [Plate 48]. The lines and surfaces of every stone can be seen with astounding clarity, from the foreground to the hills, but the water of the stream itself is an indistinct substance like milk or like the cloudy skies above. The long exposures of the view camera transform the mobile and preserve the immobile, seemingly sifting the enduring from the fleeting. In a portrait of a group of monks, those who fidget become indistinct, those who stand calmly are clear. In the image of horns in the foreground of a rocky temple, a delicate white diagonal blur is a line of prayer flags, sign of the wind moving through the landscape [Plate 38]. Connor says, "I use an 8x10 view camera because of the abundant detail and crystalline clarity of the images, and, I must admit, I also love the traditional cabinetry of the mahogany camera. I have an intuition that this camera absorbs the subject during the exposure rather than snatching it out of the environment."

Three ways in which her working method uses time differently than most contemporary photography: first of all, the cumbersome view-camera technology is one of the few survivors of a time when making photographs was a slow and arduous process; secondly, the exposures are often very long; thirdly, the prints are made by direct contact on printing-out paper (the same kind of paper Atget used, it is far less light-sensitive and therefore slower than modern papers: negative and paper are fitted into a frame and laid out in the sun of Connor's enclosed garden, where they may be exposed upward of several hours before the image is ready to be fixed). The instantaneous possibilities which make photography so appealing to the amateur are banished from her work; instead the process is painstakingly protracted, from the setting up of the camera to the printing of the image. The scene, she says, may change faster than the camera can respond to it, which dictates the nature of many of her images with people. The slowness of the camera echoes the qualities of endurance of the stones, of antiquity of the shrines she photographs, the clarity of that which remains still. The fleeting, however, is crucial in this examination of time itself, from the milky blur of moving water to the transient effects of light. Water, as a substance in almost constant change, suggests other scales of time when it accumulates as a puddle at the base of a standing stone or fills the footprints of a god. Light streams through the skylight of a room in the Himalayas like a visitation, it turns the foreground into a virtual silhouette in a desertscape, a splash of it glows almost blindingly in the dark corner of a temple where skeletons dance [Plate 47]. "Unlike the West, the dark side is more evident in Asia. Death is not hidden. Fecundity and decay are not separated from each other but rather they set into motion a creative tension and dynamic. The creator, Shiva, and the destroyer, Kali, are not opposites, but are manifestations of the same force, revolving around each other infinitely," Connor says. Images of death are recurrent in her work, and their presence calls to mind Roland Barthes' assertion that all photographs are about death in some way. Wholly imaginary works of art—paintings, novels—participate in a small-scale version of dreamtime, a time of what might have been, but photographs, however constructed, are always set in the real past—the past of yesterday in a newspaper photograph of an explosion, the past of our great-grandmothers in a Julia Margaret Cameron, but always in a here and now that is gone.

Connor's works, from the photographs of photographs to the photographs of vanished peoples' petroglyphs, are an exploration of the extent to which this past is recoverable, the extent to which the present is permeated by the past, even to the presence of the past, but the tense is always past tense. Still, her works are not elegies to what is lost but celebrations of how this past enriches the present and of how the many kinds of time nest within each other like Russian dolls or intertwine in an elaborate pattern. Each photograph becomes a talisman of other times and places, a connection to them, an altar.

Rebecca Solnit

REBECCA SOLNIT

Rebecca Solnit is the author of *Secret Exhibition: Six Artists and the California Avant-Garde of the Cold War Era* (City Lights Books, June 1990) and is currently collaborating on a book about photography, memory and landscape with artist Lewis DeSoto. In 1989 she taught a graduate seminar at the San Francisco Art Institute examining the changing relationship between visual art and the natural world and reprised the lectures for a series at the Headlands Center for the Arts, where she was writer-in-residence. A widely published essayist and critic, her current work continues this investigation of landscape and environmental art. She lives in San Francisco.

Preface
REFERENCES

Linda Connor, "Gestures of Faith," *Marks in Place* (Albuquerque: The University of New Mexico Press, 1988).

Linda Connor, "Remembering, Kathmandu," preface for her 1986 portfolio with Mark Klett.

T.S. Eliot "Tradition and the Individual Talent," *Selected Essays, 1917–1932* (New York, 1932), p. 5. Also, *Points of View* (London, 1941), pp. 25–26.

George Kubler, *The Shape of Time* (New Haven, Connecticut: Yale University Press, 1962), p. 87.

Rūmī, Mathnawī, translated by R.A. Nicholson (London: Luzac, 1926). Also, *Parabola, (The Tree of Life* edition), vol. 14, no. 3 (Fall 1989): 47.

Rebecca Solnit, "Linda Connor," *Marin Review*, vol. 11, no. 1, (Winter 1987): 8.

Spiral Journey
BIBLIOGRAPHY

Roland Barthes, *Camera Lucida* (New York: Hill and Wang, 1982).

Linda Connor, *Aperture* #93, 1982 (Esalan Conference issue).

Linda Connor, *Solos* (Millerton, New York: Apeiron Workshops, Inc., 1979).

Mircea Eliade, *The Sacred and the Profane* (New York: Harcourt, Brace and World, 1959).

Estelle Jussim and Elizabeth Lindquist-Cock, *Landscape as Photograph* (New Haven and London: Yale University Press, 1985).

Annette Kolodny, *The Lay of the Land: Metaphor as Experience and History in American Life and Letters* (Chapel Hill: University of North Carolina Press, 1984).

Ursula K. LeGuin, "A NonEuclidean View of California as a Cold Place to Be," 1982 lecture presented at University of California, San Diego, anthologized in *Dancing at the Edge of the World: Thoughts on Words, Women, Places* (New York: Grove Press, 1989).

Paul Shepard, *Nature and Madness* (San Francisco: Sierra Club Books, 1985).

Plates

SPIRAL

JOURNEY

*"Whoever wants to see the
invisible has to penetrate more deeply
into the visible"*

Robert Bly

P L A T E 1

Bureau Top

Norwalk, Connecticut, 1967

PLATE 2

Family Portraits On My
Grandmother's Bed
Stoneham, Massachusetts, 1967

PLATE 3

My Mother With Heart And Thorns

1967

PLATE 4

All American Landscape
1968

P L A T E 5

My Parents In A Basket
1969

PLATE 7

Confirmation, Chicago
1968

PLATE 10

Maine Forest

1971

PLATE 11

A Page From Jean's Book
1983

—

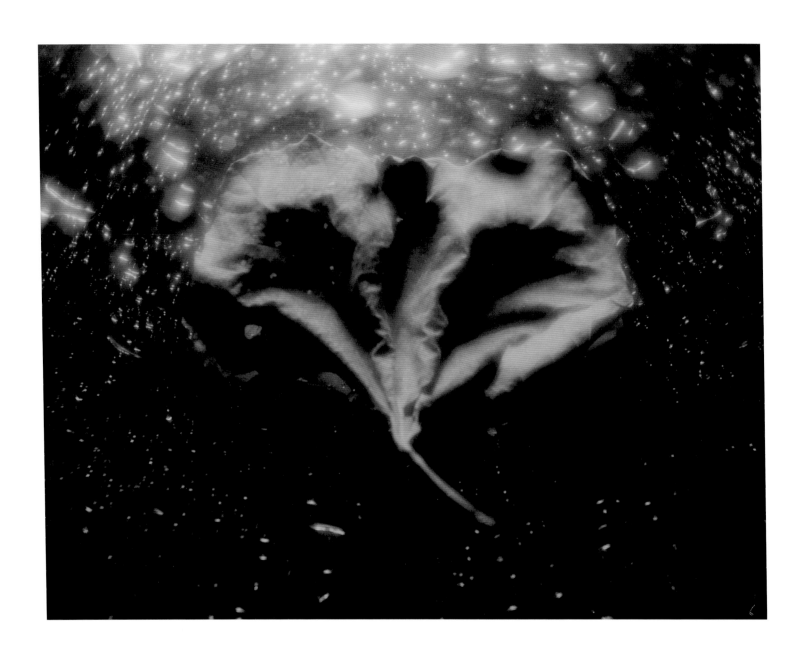

P L A T E 1 2

Leaf
1972

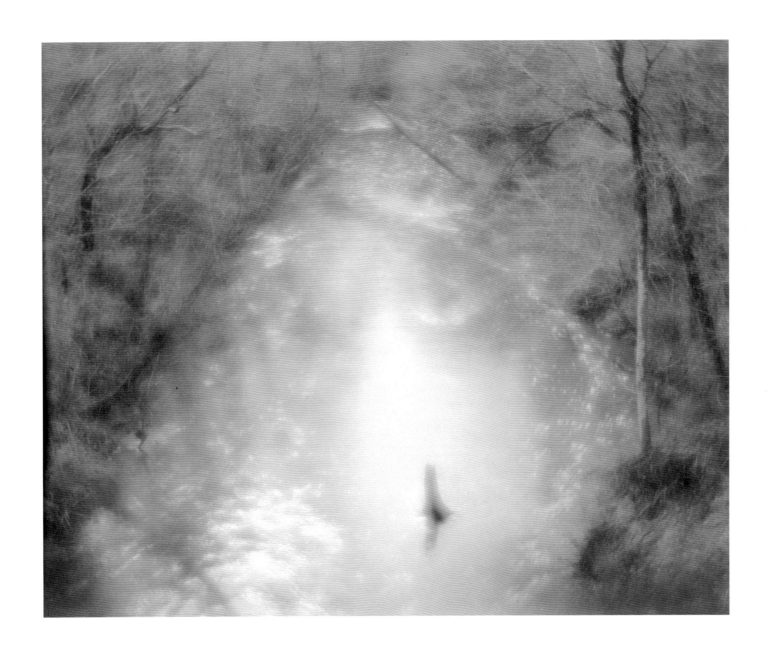

P LATE 13

River, Georgia
1977

PLATE 14

Man At Hot Springs
Baja, Mexico, 1975

PLATE 15

Foot And Hand

1975

PLATE 16

Yucatan, Mexico

1976

PLATE 17

Girl, Guatemala
1976

PLATE 18

Chairs
Yosemite, California, 1975

PLATE 19

Child's Room
1976

PLATE 20

Fish

1975

Antlers, Wyoming
1974

PLATE 22

Tree
Santa Cruz, California, 1975

PLATE 23

Nude With Net
West Indies, 1976

PLATE 24

Ceremony
Sri Lanka, 1979

PLATE 25

Kachina Kiva
Utah, 1982

PLATE 29

Moonrise
India, 1979

PLATE 31

Sora

1985

PLATE 32

Sleeping Baby
Kathmandu, Nepal, 1980

PLATE 33

Entwined Buddha
Ayuthaya, Thailand, 1988

PLATE 34

Hindu Woman With Tattoos
India, 1979

P L A T E   3 5

Dots And Hands
Fourteen Window Ruin, Utah, 1987

PLATE 36

Kapo Kohe Lele, Ancient Ceremonial Cave
For Pele, Goddess Of the Volcano
Puna, Hawaii, 1986

PLATE 37

Dolmen
France, 1989

P L A T E 3 8

Horns and Prayer Flags, Tiktse Monastery
Ladakh, India, 1985

PLATE 39

Smiling Monk
Ladakh, India, 1985

PLATE 40

Banaras, India
1979

PLATE 41

Cloud and Corral
Alta Plano, Peru, 1984

PLATE 42

Jain Nuns
India, 1979

PLATE 43

Coptic Monastery
Egypt, 1989

PLATE 44

Lotus

Kashmir, India, 1985

PLATE 45

Veiled Woman
India, 1979

PLATE 46

Hoof

Kathmandu, Nepal, 1980

PLATE 47

The Patient One, Lamayuru Monastery
Ladakh, India, 1985

PLATE 48

Black Canyon of the Gunnison
Colorado, 1987

PLATE 49

Monk's Residence
Zanskar, India, 1985